INSIDE MY BODY

BONES

WRITTEN BY EMILY C. DAWSON ILLUSTRATED BY TERESA ALBERINI

amicus
illustrated

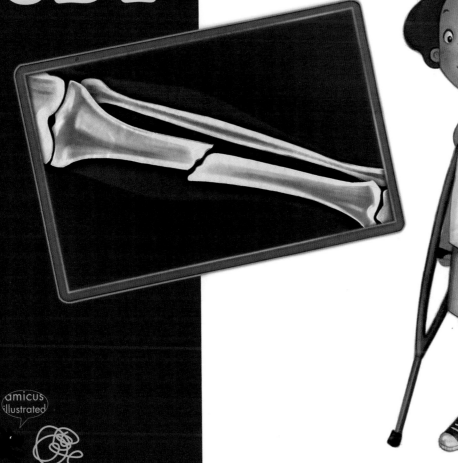

Amicus Illustrated is published by Amicus
P.O. Box 1329, Mankato, MN 56002
www.amicuspublishing.us

Library of Congress Cataloging-in-Publication Data
Dawson, Emily C.
 My bones / by Emily C. Dawson.
   pages cm. — (Inside my body)
 Includes bibliographical references and index.
 Summary: "A boy named Jack who has just broken his
leg teaches his younger sister Lissa all the things he
learned about bones while at the doctor's office getting
his cast"—Provided by publisher.
 Audience: K to grade 3.
 ISBN 978-1-60753-753-3 (library binding : alk. paper) –
 ISBN 978-1-60753-852-3 (ebook)
 1. Bones—Juvenile literature. I. Title.
 QP88.2.D39 2016
 611'.71—dc23   2014037341

Editor: Rebecca Glaser
Designer: Kathleen Petelinsek

Printed in the United States of America at
Corporate Graphics in North Mankato, Minnesota.

10 9 8 7 6 5 4 3 2 1

ABOUT THE AUTHOR

Emily C. Dawson has loved reading, writing,
and basically everything about books since
she was in grade school. She has written
more than 40 books for young readers and
enjoys making educational topics easy to
understand and fun to read.

ABOUT THE ILLUSTRATOR

Teresa Alberini has always loved painting
and drawing. She attended the Academy
of Fine Arts in Florence, Italy, and she now
lives and works as an illustrator in a small
town on the Italian coast. Visit her on the
web at www.teresaalberini.com.

"Hi, Jack! Did the doctor fix your leg?"

"No, Lissa. It's broken. My dirt bike fell on it hard."

"But now you get crutches!"

"And this hard cast. It will keep the bone in place while it grows back together."

"The bone will fix itself?"

"Yes, in a month or two. And check out this poster."

"Wow. How many bones are there? 100?"

"Even more. An adult body has 206 bones."

"But what about my body?"

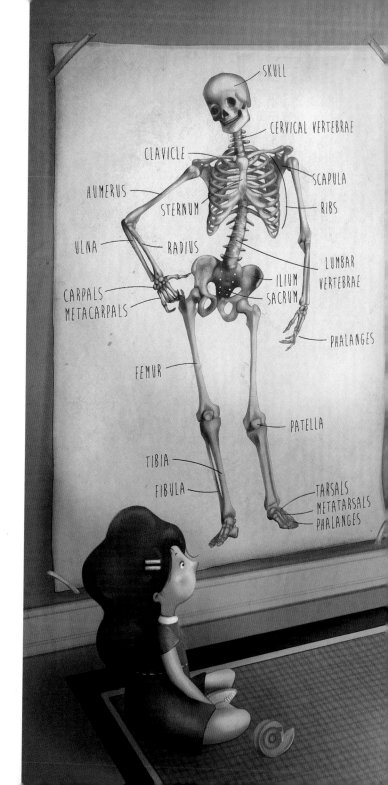

"When you're born, you have 300 bones. Some bones start as smaller pieces. They grow together as you get older."

"The skeleton looks just like my Halloween costume, Jack."

"It's more than a costume, Lissa. Your skeleton gives you shape and holds you up."

"Hee-hee."

"What's so funny, Lissa?"

"Without bones, we'd be blobs."

"Yep. We'd have no leg bones to walk. And no jawbone to chew or talk."

"And we'd look like silly blob monsters!"

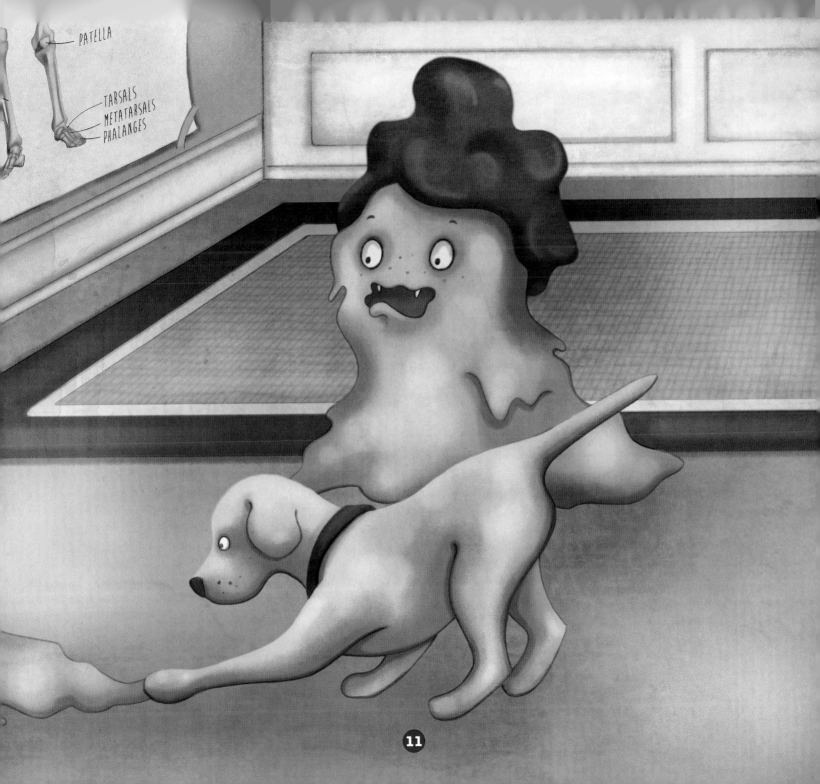

PATELLA

TARSALS
METATARSALS
PHALANGES

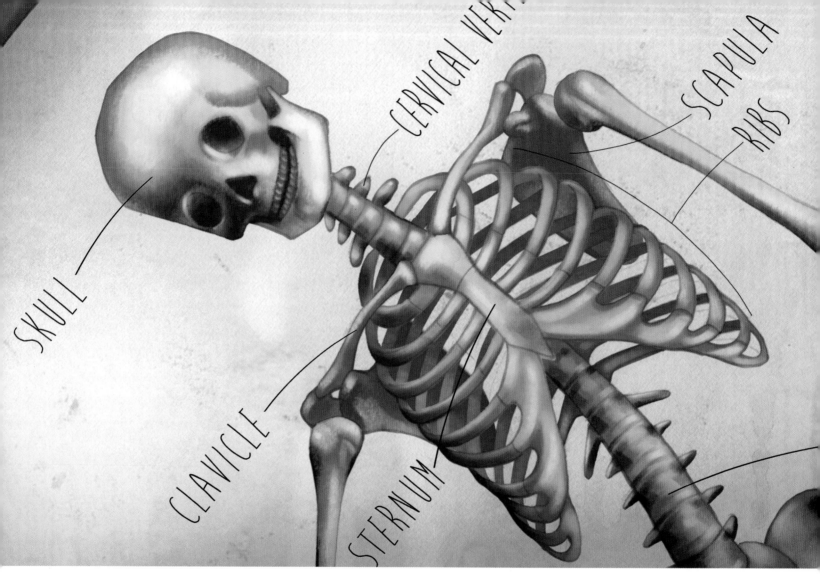

SKULL

CLAVICLE

STERNUM

CERVICAL VERT...

SCAPULA

RIBS

"Luckily, we're not silly blob monsters."

"Those bones look like a cage."

"That's the rib cage. It protects your heart and lungs."

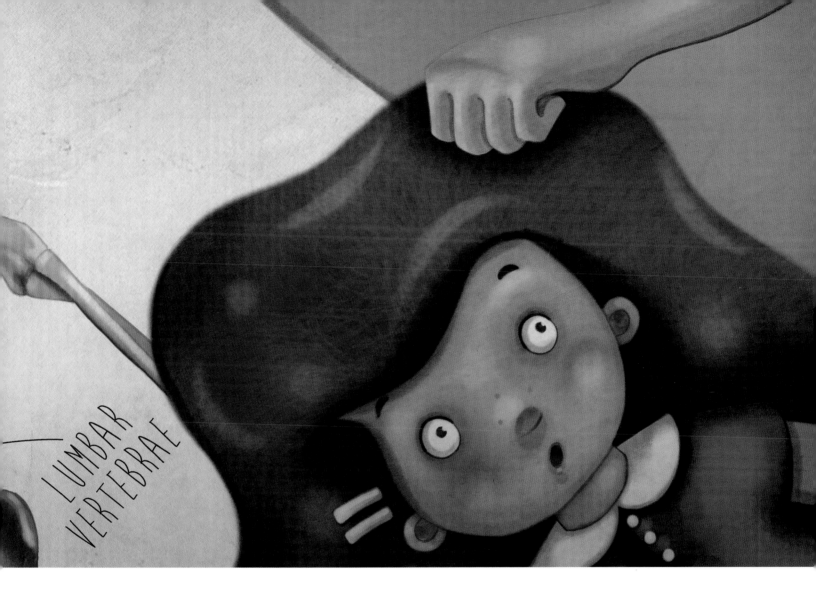

"So my bones have a job. They keep my insides safe!"

"Yep! Just like your hard skull protects your brain!"

"But if bones are so hard, Jack, how can we move?"

"Your muscles move the bones at joints, where two bones meet. Your knee joint lets your leg bend."

"Look at my shoulder. My arm moves in circles!"

"Hey, watch out!"

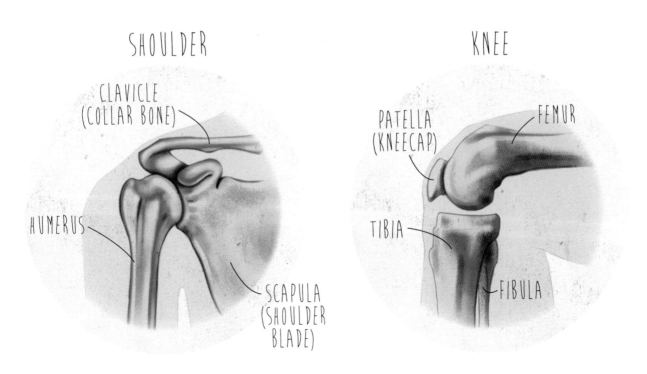

SHOULDER

CLAVICLE
(COLLAR BONE)

HUMERUS

SCAPULA
(SHOULDER
BLADE)

KNEE

PATELLA
(KNEECAP)

FEMUR

TIBIA

FIBULA

"My back bends this far. See what I learned in gymnastics?"

"Wow, Lissa! You can bend and twist your spine, or backbone, because it has so many small bones."

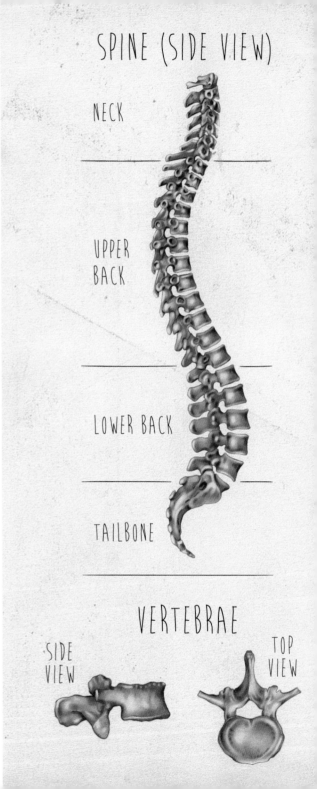

SPINE (SIDE VIEW)

NECK

UPPER BACK

LOWER BACK

TAILBONE

VERTEBRAE

SIDE VIEW

TOP VIEW

"Are the spine bones the smallest?"

"No, the smallest bones are inside your ear. But your feet and hands have lots of small bones too."

"So I can play piano! Or grab blocks with my toes."

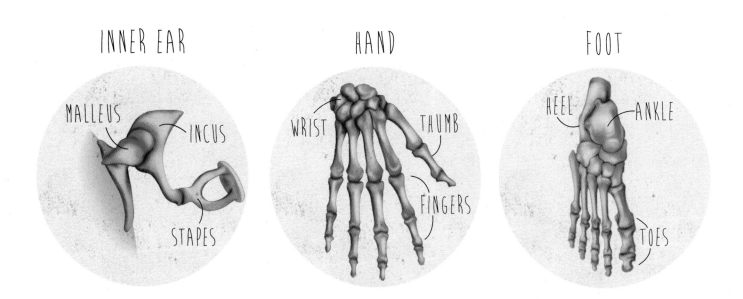

INNER EAR

MALLEUS

INCUS

STAPES

HAND

WRIST

THUMB

FINGERS

FOOT

HEEL

ANKLE

TOES

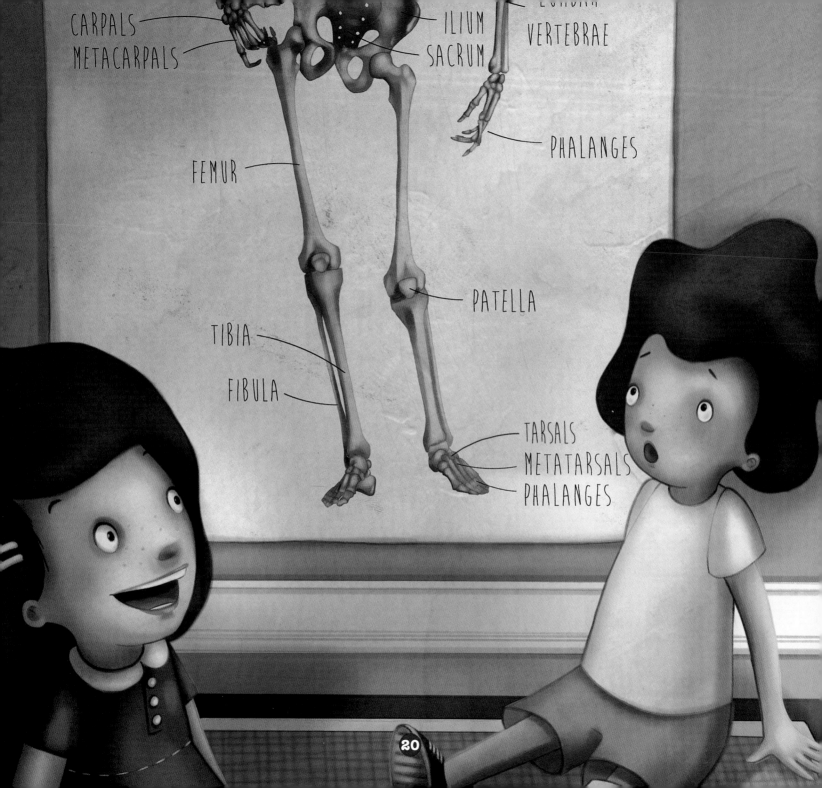

"Which bone is the biggest, Jack?"

"Will you ever stop asking questions?"

"No."

"The femur is the biggest—and strongest."

"Which bone did you break?"

"The tibia. It's strong too, but even strong bones can break."

"That's why mom always gives us milk, Lissa. Milk has calcium, which keeps your bones strong."

"Then let's have milk and cookies!"

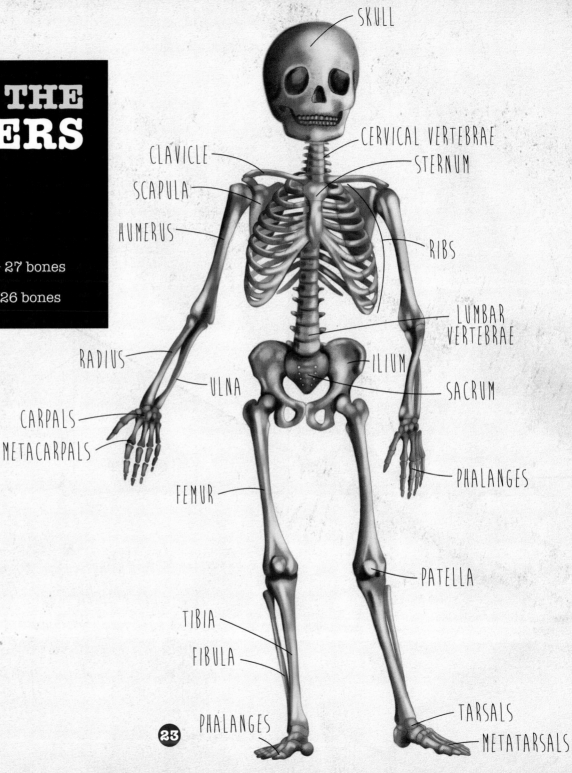

BODY BY THE NUMBERS

Skull – 22 bones

Rib cage – 24 bones

Spine – 33 bones

Hand (including wrist) – 27 bones

Foot (including ankle) – 26 bones

SKULL

CLAVICLE

SCAPULA

CERVICAL VERTEBRAE

STERNUM

HUMERUS

RIBS

LUMBAR VERTEBRAE

RADIUS

ILIUM

ULNA

SACRUM

CARPALS

METACARPALS

PHALANGES

FEMUR

PATELLA

TIBIA

FIBULA

TARSALS

PHALANGES

METATARSALS

23

GLOSSARY

joint—A place where two bones meet.

skeleton—The framework of bones that supports and protects your body.

skull—The bony framework of the head that protects the brain.

spine—The row of connected bones that goes down the middle of your back.

READ MORE

Ballard, Carol. **What Happens to Broken Bones?** Inside My Body. Chicago: Raintree, 2011.

Herrington, Lisa M. **I Broke My Arm**. New York: Children's Press, 2015

Tieck, Sarah. **Skeletal System**. Body Systems. Edina, Minn.: ABDO Pub., 2011.

Wood, Lily. **Skeletons**. New York: Scholastic, 2011.

WEBSITES

The Children's University of Manchester: The Skeleton
www.childrensuniversity.manchester.ac.uk/interactives/science/bodyandmedicine/theskeleton/
View interactive slides that explain the skeletal system and how your bones work.

eSKELETONS: Life Size Printout
eskeletons.org/sites/eskeletons.org/files//files/resources/000646791.pdf
Print and put together a life-size picture of a child's skeleton.

Idaho Public Television Dialogue for Kids: The Skeleton Facts
idahoptv.org/dialogue4kids/season13/skeletons/facts.cfm
Read cool facts about bones and scroll over highlighted words to learn new "bone" vocabulary.

KidsHealth: Your Bones
kidshealth.org/kid/htbw/bones.html#
Read about what makes up your bones and see a diagram of what's inside your bones.

Every effort has been made to ensure that these websites are appropriate for children. However, because of the nature of the Internet, it is impossible to guarantee that these sites will remain active indefinitely or that their contents will not be altered.